PEACHTREE

Darwin

by Alice B. McGinty

illustrated by Mary Azarian

HOUGHTON MIFFLIN BOOKS FOR CHILDREN
Houghton Mifflin Harcourt
Boston 2009

From the time he was young until long after his beard grew white, Charles Darwin loved to collect things. He collected rocks from the English countryside he explored as a boy, coins in the home where he grew up, shells from trips to the sea, and dead bugs, too.

Charles thought about the things he collected, learned their names, and labeled each one.

It was soon after I began collecting stones . . . that I distinctly recollect the desire I had of being able to know something about every pebble in front of the hall door.

When Charles was just eight years old, his mother died, leaving him, his brother, and four sisters. Their father, a kind but busy doctor, soon sent Charles to a boarding school near their country home.

At Shrewsbury School, Charles discovered that he would much rather be exploring than studying Greek or Latin. As often as he could, he ran home during his free time. He fished and read, and, when he got older, he hunted too.

One of the things Charles liked best was helping his older brother Erasmus do chemistry experiments in the toolshed by their home. The gases and concoctions Charles made with his brother earned him the nickname "Gas."

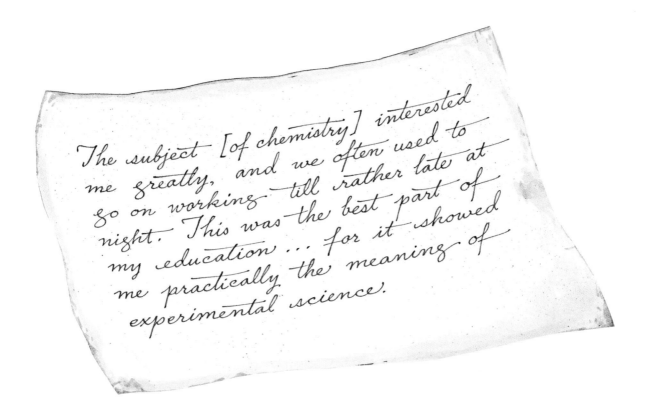

The subject [of chemistry] interested me greatly, and we often used to go on working till rather late at night. This was the best part of my education ... for it showed me practically the meaning of experimental science.

The headmaster at school became angry with Charles for spending his time on experiments instead of schoolwork. Charles was doing so poorly in school, in fact, that his father pulled him out when he was sixteen years old and sent him to join Erasmus, who had gone off to Edinburgh University to study medicine. Charles would study medicine, too, his father decided, and become a doctor.

Charles found medical school dull, though, and unpleasant. When he had to watch an operation, he ran away before it was done. After only two years, his father took him out of medical school and sent him to Cambridge University to become a pastor.

To my deep mortification my father once said to me, "You care for nothing but shooting, dogs, and rat-catching, and you will be a disgrace to yourself and all your family." But my father, who was the kindest man I ever knew, and whose memory I love with all my heart, must have been angry and somewhat unjust when he used such words.

Though Charles believed in God and the Bible, he thought the classes that prepared him to be a pastor were just as dull as those in medical school. Instead of studying, he collected beetles and went to lectures about botany. Charles became good friends with the lecturer, the Reverend Professor Henslow. During long walks, the professor taught Charles not only about plants, but about the branches of science that studied animals and rocks as well.

After Charles graduated from Cambridge, cramming hard for his final tests to please his father, a most unexpected chance came along. A letter arrived from Professor Henslow asking if Charles wanted to sail on a ship leaving soon for South America to map the coast. Would Charles go on the voyage to be a friend to the captain and a naturalist to study the plants and animals they discovered? Would he ever!

But Charles's father said no. "A wild scheme," he said of the trip.

His father, however, must have seen how Charles longed to go, for he added, "If you can find any man of common sense who advises you to go I will give my consent." So, Charles showed his uncle, Josiah Wedgwood, a list of his father's objections:

1) Disreputable to my character as a Clergyman

2) A wild scheme

3) That they must have offered to many others before me the place of Naturalist

4) And from its not being accepted there must be some serious objection to the vessel or expedition

5) That I should never settle down to a steady life hereafter

6) That my accommodations would be most uncomfortable

7) That you should consider it as again changing my profession

8) That it would be a useless undertaking

When Uncle Josiah wrote a letter to Dr. Darwin arguing each objection in turn, Charles's father finally said yes. Charles could go.

Charles went to London to meet the captain, who later took him to Plymouth to tour the ship. Captain FitzRoy, an unusual man, almost decided not to take Charles on the voyage. Why? As Charles writes, "on account of the shape of my nose!"

[Captain FitzRoy] was convinced that he could judge of a man's character by the outline of his features; and he doubted whether anyone with my nose could possess sufficient energy and determination for the voyage. But I think he was afterwards well satisfied that my nose had spoken falsely.

In 1831, Charles Darwin set sail on the HMS *Beagle*, beginning what would become a five-year trip around the world. Seasick, he got off at every stop. He explored islands and coasts. He followed rivers. He climbed mountains and hiked though tropical rainforests. What Charles saw filled him with awe and left him believing firmly in a God who had created these wonders.

It is easy to specify the individual objects of admiration in these grand scenes; but it is not possible to give an adequate idea of the higher feelings of wonder, astonishment, and devotion, which fill and elevate the mind.

Everywhere he went, Charles collected fossils and plants, insects, birds, and animals. Just as he had done as a child, he learned the names of the things he'd collected—though some were brand new to science and not even named. He labeled as many of them as he could. Charles didn't have much time to think about his collections, though. There was too much to do: measuring a baobab tree on the Cape Verde Islands off the coast of Africa, unearthing a huge fossil skull in Argentina, and exploring islands and ports up and down the coast of South America.

Charles sent his notes and collections to Professor Henslow in England, knowing he would think about them later when he returned.

Rio De Janeiro, Brazil
May 18, 1832

My Dear Henslow,

... On the coast I collected many marine animals... I took several specimens of an Octopus, which possessed a most marvellous power of changing its colours; equalling any chameleon, and evidently accommodating the changes to the colour of the ground which it passed over....

Yours affectionately
Chas. Darwin

Octopus Vulgaris

Bracypelma Smithi

Wherever Charles went, he studied the geology of the land to learn about Earth's history and how it was changing. What did it mean when he found seashells high on a mountain, 350 feet above the sea? Or when bands of rock had been mysteriously twisted? On his journey, he discovered the teeth and bones of animals long extinct. He saw for himself how an earthquake shivered solid rock and how an erupting volcano reshaped the land.

There is nothing like Geology; the pleasure of the first day's partridge shooting or first day's hunting cannot be compared to finding a fine group of fossil bones, which tell their story of former times with almost a living tongue.

It was geology that first excited Charles about stopping at the Galápagos Islands near the end of his voyage. These islands of black volcanic rocks, huge tame tortoises, and creeping lizards would give Charles many new volcanoes to explore and unique plants and animals to collect.

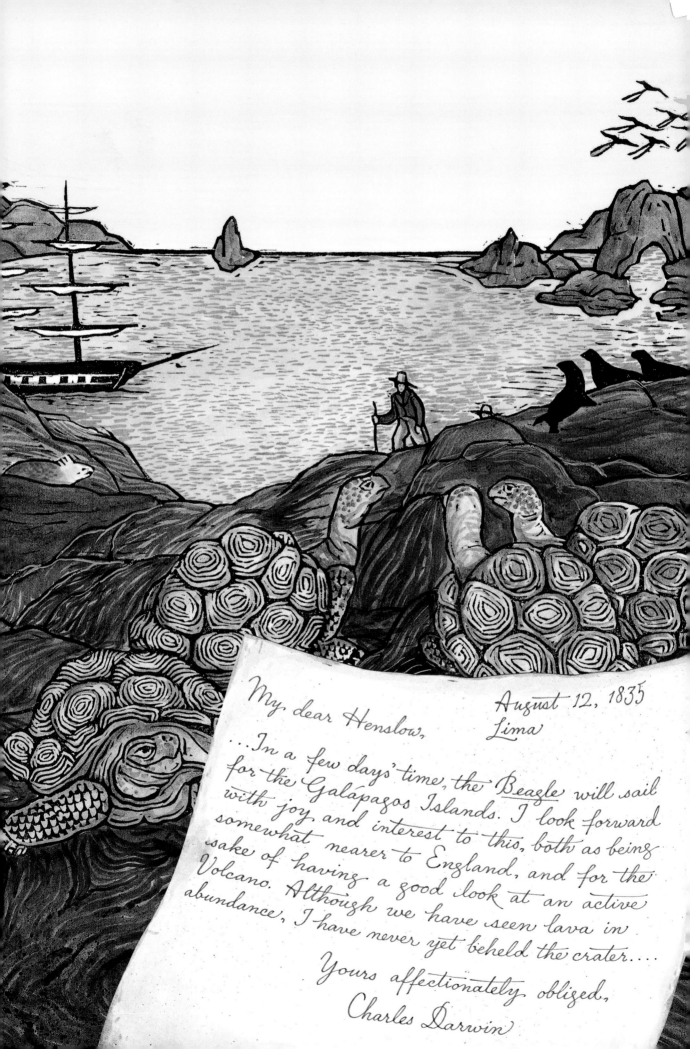

My dear Henslow,   August 12, 1835
                                     Lima

...In a few days' time, the Beagle will sail
for the Galápagos Islands. I look forward
with joy and interest to this, both as being
somewhat nearer to England, and for the
sake of having a good look at an active
Volcano. Although we have seen lava in
abundance, I have never yet beheld the crater....

Yours affectionately obliged,
Charles Darwin

However, it would be the birds he collected on the Galápagos Islands—which he thought to be a mixed group of finches, blackbirds, grosbeaks, and a wren—that would later give Charles Darwin the surprise of his life.

As the *Beagle* crossed the Pacific and circled the world toward home, Charles sat in his tiny cabin writing and arranging his notes. After almost five years, he was seasick and homesick and ready to get back to England . . . but what would he find there? Would he be accepted as a scientist? Would other scientists find his unusual collections worthwhile?

April 29, 1836

Port Lewis, Mauritius

My dear [sister] Caroline,

. . . I assure you I look forward with no little anxiety to the time when Henslow, putting on a grave face, shall decide on the merits of my notes. If he shakes his head in a disapproving manner, I shall then know that I had better at once give up science, for science will have given up me. For I have worked with every grain of energy I possess. . . .

Your affectionate brother,

Chas. Darwin

To Charles's amazement, when he came back to England, many scientists already knew his name. Professor Henslow had been sharing his letters and collections with them. Charles Darwin, budding naturalist, had begun to earn their respect. Charles gave his collections to these experts: the plants to botanists, fossils to paleontologists, the birds to an ornithologist. They would examine his specimens to help him understand what he'd found.

In rooms he'd rented in London, Charles wrote about his travels, met new scientists, and waited for the experts' reply. When the ornithologist John Gould shared what he'd learned about the birds from the Galápagos Islands, the news shocked Charles. The mixed collection of birds—which Charles had labeled as finches, blackbirds, grosbeaks, and a wren—were actually *all* finches. Each was a closely related kind, or species, of finch. The similar structure of the birds' beaks and bodies, their short tails, and their feathers proved that they were related, Mr. Gould said.

Charles was astonished. Some of these birds had long beaks. Some had short beaks. Some had thin beaks and some thick. How could they *all* be finches?

Charles thought carefully about what this discovery meant. Why were there so many species of finches on these islands? Had all of them been around since the world began?

Or had the finches come from the same ancestors and changed?

FINCHES of the GALÁPAGOS
collected by C. Darwin

C. fusca
C. olivacea
G. fortis
G. pallida
G. scandens
C. parvulus
G. fuliginosa
G. conirostris
C. pauper

This idea of change went against everything Charles had been taught. Charles believed that God had created each kind of plant and animal in the world, just as the Bible said.

Could new species of plants and animals form on their own? The Bible seemed to say that it could not be so.

Yet as Charles examined his collections and as information came in from the experts, the evidence seemed to show that species *did* change over time. The fossils he'd found in

Argentina came from huge creatures that were closely related to smaller ones that now lived there. Had the giant skull he'd found come from an ancestor of a modern armadillo? More and more, it seemed to Charles that the fossil creatures and the finches had changed to form new species.

Charles wrote down his observations and questions about species in a special notebook, but he kept his notebook secret. Would people think that he did not believe in the Bible? Speaking out against the church was blasphemy, and for some it had meant jail.

Because he was a scientist, Charles kept working to understand what he'd found, but he did not tell a soul.

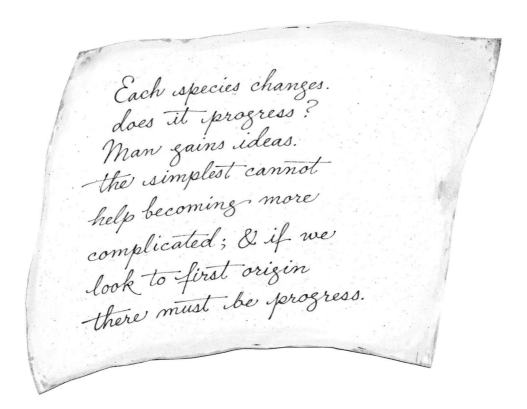

*Each species changes.
does it progress?
Man gains ideas.
the simplest cannot
help becoming more
complicated; & if we
look to first origin
there must be progress.*

Some people wonder if it was worrying about these secrets that made Charles Darwin sick so often after his journey. He had headaches and heart tremors and stomach problems and nobody knew why. Even after his marriage and his move to the quiet English countryside, sometimes Charles felt so sick that he couldn't work at all. More often, though, he found

that his work made him forget his pain, so he kept at it, surrounded by his growing family.

Day after day, Charles added to his secret notebook, filling it and then others. His biggest question was this: If species did change, how did it happen?

It was a book Charles said he read for fun, about how the number of people in the world grew, that led him to an answer. The book said that the population of the world could not keep growing because food would run out and people would starve. Charles realized that the same was true for animals. There were more animals born than could survive. It would be the strongest of each species, those most able to find food and escape from enemies, that would survive.

This gave him a theory that could explain how species changed. Here's how his theory worked:

A giraffe born with a longer neck could reach food higher in the trees and survive during hard times when food was scarce.

A deer who ran fastest would escape its enemies.

The fast deer and the long-necked giraffe were most fit to survive, and they would pass those traits—the faster legs or the longer neck—to their offspring. Deer who were slower and giraffes with shorter necks would die.

It at once struck me that under these circumstances favorable variations would tend to be preserved, and unfavorable ones to be destroyed. The result of this would be the formation of new species.

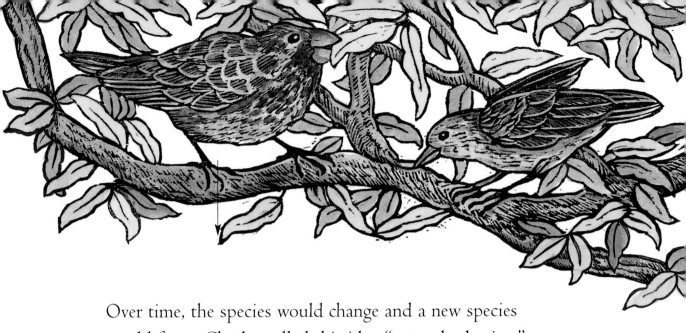

Over time, the species would change and a new species
would form. Charles called this idea "natural selection."
Later, it would be called "survival of the fittest."

Charles's theory also explained the differences in the finches from the Galápagos Islands. Those born with thicker
beaks could crack open bigger, tougher seeds. Those with
thinner beaks could eat smaller seeds, or reach insects under
the bark of trees. Over time, the thick-beaked finches had
some babies with even thicker, stronger beaks. The thin-
beaked finches had some babies with thinner, longer beaks.
It was these finches who survived, because they could
find food even in the hardest times.

The finches had come from the same ancestors,
but each one had slowly changed to form many new
species of finches. These species, which included
cactus finches, ground finches, and tree finches, were
closely related, but each one was specially adapted to
find its own food.

Charles wrote out his theory, arranging his thoughts on scribbled pages. Though he kept these pages secret, he knew if he ever wanted to publish his theory, he should discuss his ideas with other scientists. Finally, more than seven years after his voyage, he decided it was time. With caution, he mentioned the idea that species could change in a letter to J. D. Hooker, a young botanist who had been examining his plants from the Galápagos Islands.

January 11, 1844 — Down Bromley Kent

My Dear Sir,

. . . At last gleams of light have come, and I am almost convinced (quite contrary to the opinion I started with) that species are not (it is like confessing a murder) immutable . . . I think I have found out (here's presumption!) the simple way by which species become exquisitely adapted to various ends. . . .

Believe me my dear Sir.

Very truly yours,

C. Darwin

A few weeks later J. D. Hooker responded. He said that he, too, believed that species could change. "I shall be delighted to hear how you think that this change may have taken place," he wrote to Charles.

Charles must have been relieved to read this. Still, sharing his theory with others could bring disgrace to him and his family. Although he hoped one day to publish his theory, he shared it now only with his closest friends.

Charles passed the years working in the study of Down House, his country home, and building on his theory. He studied barnacles, classifying each species. He raised pigeons to learn how traits were passed from parents to offspring. He did experiments to support his theory, sometimes with his whole family helping (by now, he and his wife, Emma, had ten children).

One of Charles's children remembers:

The love of experiment was very strong in him, and I can remember the way he would say, "I shan't be easy till I have tried it," as if an outside force were driving him.

—Francis Darwin

Although his friends urged him to publish his work, Charles still did not feel ready. But when a young scientist, Alfred Russel Wallace, came up with ideas very much like Charles's own, Charles's friends told him he *must* publish his work.

In 1859, Charles published *The Origin of the Species* and braced himself for the worst. Would people say his work was not complete? Would they believe he was speaking out against the church?

Indeed, there were attacks:

Cambridge, December 24, 1859

My Dear Darwin

...I have read your book with more pain than pleasure. Parts of it I admired greatly, parts I laughed at till my sides were almost sore; other parts I read with absolute sorrow; because I think them utterly false and grievously mischievous....

... your true-hearted old friend,

A. Sedgwick

Even Charles's old friend Professor Henslow told him politely that he didn't agree with everything Charles had written. Still, in public, Professor Henslow defended Charles's right to question the origin of living things.

Other close friends supported Charles fully. J. D. Hooker, the very first person with whom Charles had shared his theory, wrote to him, "I am perfectly tired of marvelling at the wonderful amount of facts you have brought to bear, and your skill in marshalling them."

Another said, "No work on Natural History Science I have met with has made so great an impression upon me . . . Depend upon it you have earned the lasting gratitude of all thoughtful men."

Charles, whose illness became worse in times of conflict, stayed at home and relied on his friends to defend his theory to the world.

Ilkley, Yorkshire
December 2 [1859]

My dear Lyell
. . . I fully believe that I owe the comfort of the next few years of my life to your generous support and that of a very few others. I do not think I am brave enough to have stood being odious without support; now I feel as bold as a Lion. . . .

Yours most truly,
C. Darwin

Charles's book sold out quickly, over a thousand copies and then many more. Over the years, it would sell millions of copies around the world.

ORANGUTAN
Pongo pyymueus
BORNEO

Charles knew, though, that his work on species was not done.
After looking through his secret notebooks at the descriptions
of natives he'd seen on his journey and an orangutan he'd seen
at a London zoo, he dove into his research again and wrote
The Descent of Man. This book took his species theory one
step further and showed how humans as a species could have
changed, or evolved, from the same ancestors as apes. Charles
Darwin called his idea evolution.

Some people were offended by the idea of being related to apes. They argued that humans were created specially by God. Charles himself finally came to believe that there were no answers to his questions about God. He saw the universe as too amazing not to have been created by a God. He also believed, though, in his theories. His life's work had shown that all living things, including people, are part of a natural, changing world.

There is grandeur in this view of life, with its
several powers, having been originally breathed by
the Creator into a few forms or into one; and that,
whilst this planet has gone cycling on according

to the fixed law of gravity, from so simple a beginning endless forms most beautiful and wonderful have been, and are being, evolved.

$\mathcal{I}$N 1882, SEVENTY-THREE YEARS AFTER HIS BIRTH IN 1809, Charles Darwin died. More than one hundred years after his death, some people still argue over his ideas. More and more people, though, have found that their religious beliefs and Darwin's discoveries can exist side by side.

What began for Charles Darwin as scribbled thoughts in a secret notebook led to ideas that have forever changed how we see the world. Now, when a young collector picks up a beetle, or learns the name of a bird, he or she can believe that the living thing has evolved over millions of years to become what it is today.

Whenever I have found out that I have blundered, or that my work has been imperfect, and when I have been contemptuously criticized, and even when I have been overpraised, so that I have felt mortified, it has been my greatest comfort to say hundreds of times to myself... "I have worked as hard and as well as I could, and no man can do more than this."

Charles Darwin [signature]

Author's Note

Perhaps Charles Darwin did not realize that he would come to be known as one of the greatest thinkers in science. He wrote his autobiography for his children, with no thought that it would ever be published. Humble, but with great ambition, this thoughtful, quiet scientist wrote many books in his lifetime, contributed great new ideas to science, and changed the way people everywhere understand life on Earth. Using only the simplest equipment in his experiments and relying on observation and logic, Charles Darwin showed just how much can be accomplished by simply asking a question and working diligently to find the answer.

Notes

Quotes in the book (in sequential order) come from the following sources:

"It was soon after": Charles Darwin, *Charles Darwin and the Voyage of the* Beagle,
ed. Nora Barlow (New York: Philosophical Library, Inc., 1946), 14.
Hereafter cited as *Voyage*.

"The subject [of chemistry]": Charles Darwin, *Charles Darwin's Autobiography, With
His Notes and Letters Depicting the Growth of the Origin of Species*, ed. Sir
Francis Darwin (New York: Henry Schuman, 1950), 19. Hereafter cited as
Autobiography.

"To my deep mortification": *Autobiography*, 17.

"A wild scheme" and list of objections: Charles Darwin to R. W. Darwin, August 31
1831, in *Voyage*, 26.

"If you can find any man": *Autobiography*, 36.

"on account of the shape": *Autobiography*, 36.

"[Captain FitzRoy] was convinced": *Autobiography*, 36.

"It is easy to specify": Charles Darwin, *Journal of Researches into the Natural History
and Geology of the Countries Visited During the Voyage of H.M.S.* Beagle *Round
the World, Under the Command of Capt. Fitz Roy, R.N.* 2nd ed. (London:

John Murray, 1845), Rio De Janiero, April 18, 1832, 26.

"On the coast": Charles Darwin to J. S. Henslow, May 18, 1832, in "Extracts from
Letters Addressed to Professor Henslow" (Read at a meeting of the Cambridge
Philosophical Society, November 16, 1835, privately printed, 1835), 4.

"There is nothing like Geology": Charles Darwin to Catherine Darwin, April 6, 1834, in
Voyage, 96.

"In a few days' time": Charles Darwin to J. S. Henslow, August 12, 1835, in *More Letters of
Charles Darwin. A Record of His Work in a Series of Hitherto Unpublished
Letters*, vol. 1, ed. Francis Darwin and A. C. Seward (London: John Murray, 1903), 26.

"I assure you": Charles Darwin to Caroline Darwin, April 29, 1836, in *Voyage*, 138.

"Each species changes": Charles Darwin. "Notebook B: (Transmutation of species
[1837–1838])," 18.

"It at once struck me": *Autobiography*, 54.

"At last gleams of light": Charles Darwin to J. D. Hooker, January 11, 1844, in *The Life
and Letters of Charles Darwin, Including an Autobiographical Chapter*, vol. 2, ed.
Francis Darwin (London: John Murray, 1887), 23. Hereafter cited as
Life and Letters.

"I shall be delighted to hear": J. D. Hooker to Charles Darwin, January 29, 1844, in
Darwin Correspondence Project, www.darwinproject.ac.uk (accessed September 5, 2007).

"The love of experiment": Francis Darwin, "Reminiscences of My Father's Everyday
Life," in *Autobiography*, 109.

"I have read your book": Adam Sedgwick to Charles Darwin, November 24, 1859, in
Life and Letters, 248.

"I am perfectly tired": J. D. Hooker to Charles Darwin, December 12, 1859, in *Life and
Letters*, 242.

"No work on Natural History": T. H. Huxley to Charles Darwin, November 23, 1859,
in *Life and Letters*, 231.

"I fully believe": Charles Darwin to C. Lyell, December 2, 1859, in *Life and Letters*, 238.

"There is grandeur": Charles Darwin, *The Origin of Species*, 6th ed. (London: John
Murray, 1872), 429.

"Whenever I have found": *Autobiography*, 58.

Additional Books Consulted:

Browne, Janet. *Voyaging*. New York: Alfred A. Knopf, 1995.

———. *The Power of Place*. New York: Alfred A. Knopf, 2002.

Darwin, Charles. *The Autobiography of Charles Darwin, 1809–1882, with Original
Omissions Restored*. Edited by Nora Barlow. New York: Harcourt Brace and
Company, 1958.

Internet Resources:

The Complete Work of Charles Darwin Online: http://darwin-online.org.uk.

For my father, Saul Blumenthal
— A.B.M.

To the memory of Selkie and Hilda,
two of the most evolved beings I have known.
— M.A.

The author wishes to thank Dr. Richard W. Burkhardt, professor emeritus,
Department of History, University of Illinois, for his expertise and fact-checking.

Text copyright © 2009 by Alice B. McGinty
Illustrations copyright © 2009 by Mary Azarian

Houghton Mifflin Books for Children is an imprint
of Houghton Mifflin Harcourt Publishing Company.

www.hmhbooks.com

The text of this book is set in Centaur.
The illustrations are woodcuts hand-tinted with watercolors.
Calligraphy by Leah Palmer Preiss

Library of Congress Cataloging-in-Publication Data
McGinty, Alice B.
Darwin / by Alice B. McGinty ; illustrated by Mary Azarian.
p. cm.
ISBN 978-0-618-99531-8
1. Darwin, Charles, 1809–1882—Juvenile literature. 2. Naturalists—England—Biography—
Juvenile literature. I. Azarian, Mary, ill. II. Title.
QH31.D2M38 2009
576.8'2092—dc22
[B]
2008033930

Printed in Singapore
TWP 10 9 8 7 6 5 4 3 2 1